Are You Ready?

The Ultimate Guide to AI Business Trends and Future Careers

First Edition

Volume I

Shahdrick William Samson

First Edition published in June 2023

Copyright © 2023 National Career Development Center

ISBN: 979-8-89074-430-2

Are You Ready?

All rights reserved. No part of this book may be reproduced, stored or transmitted in any form or by any means, electronic or mechanical, including photocopy or any retrieval system, without prior permission in written from the publisher. For permission requests, contact: info@samsonna.com

Legal Disclaimer

The book contains personal experiences, research, and speculation based on experiences and research. While every effort has been made to ensure the accuracy of the information provided in this book, the information does not constitute a recommendation and is without any representation or warranty, expressed or implied.

Neither the author nor the publisher can be held liable or responsible for any direct, indirect, or consequential damages resulting from its use, reliability, accuracy or completeness and the information cannot be guaranteed. It is important to note that this book does not create a consultant-client relationship between the author and the reader.

DEDICATION

I dedicate this book to my beloved family and friends.

To my extraordinary father, whose support has been the cornerstone of my life and success, I offer my deepest appreciation. I am also thankful to my loving wife, Sana and children, whose encouragement has inspired me to strive for greater achievements and make a meaningful contribution to society.

Are You Ready?

Contents

Introduction 8
Chapter 1: Understand the Fundamentals of AI and its Implications 13
   1.1. Fundamentals of AI 13
   1.2. Explosive Development of AI 15
   1.3. Disruption in Multiple Industries creating New Opportunities 17
      1.3.1. Artificial Intelligence in Business 17
      1.3.2. Artificial Intelligence in Healthcare 21
      1.3.3. Artificial Intelligence in Pharmaceutical 22
      1.3.4. Artificial Intelligence in the Financial Services Industry 22
      1.3.5. Artificial Intelligence in Transportation 24
      1.3.6. Artificial Intelligence in Education 25
   1.4. Implications and Challenges 27
      1.4.1. Impact on the Job Market 27
      1.4.2. Ethical Considerations 29
Chapter 2: Discover and Embrace the Future of AI 31
   1.1. AI Advancements causing Global Disruption 31
   1.2. High Demand Careers and Businesses of the Future 32
      1.2.1. Cybersecurity 32
      1.2.2. Data Analysis and Science 36
      1.2.3. Renewable Energy 39
      1.2.4. Augmented and Virtual Reality (VR/AR) 43
      1.2.5. Telemedicine and Healthcare 47
      Roles in Remote Healthcare and Telemedicine 48
      Factors for Success 50
      Future Prospects 51
      1.2.6. E-commerce and Digital Marketing 52
Chapter 3: Evaluate Your Interests and Strengths 58
   1.1. Identify Your Passion and Interest within IT 61
      1.1.1. Explore Different Specializations 61
      1.1.2. Reflect on Your Skills and Aptitudes 61
      1.1.3. Consider Personal Interests 62
      1.1.4. Seek Experiences and Exposure 62
   1.2. Technical Skills Assessment: 64
   1.3. Education and Training 64

1.4. Practical Experience: 65
1.5. Seek Feedback: 65
1.6. Determine any Gaps in Your Skill-set and Areas for Improvement: 66
1.7. Analyze Requirements for Potential Jobs 67
1.8. Research Industry Trends: 67
1.9. Seek Learning Opportunities: 68
1.10. Seek Mentorship and Guidance 68
1.11. Embrace a Growth Mindset 69
1.12. Conduct Informational Interviews 69
1.13. Utilize Online Resources 69
1.14. Seek Guidance from Career Counselors or Mentors 70
1.15. Consider Your Long-Term Goals 70
1.16. Industry Outlook 71
1.17. Salary and Compensation 72
1.18. Emerging Technologies and Trends 72
1.19. Skill Transferability and Flexibility 73
1.20. Continuously Adapt and Evolve 73

Chapter 4: Choose your Path 75
1.1. Determine Necessary Competencies 75
1.2. Pick a Respected Degree Program 76
1.3. Look into Your IT Certification Courses 76
1.4. Think About Online Immersive Training 77
1.5. Explore Educational and Training Options 77
1.6. Never Stop Studying 78

Chapter 5: Equip Yourself 79
1.1. Cooperative Education and Internships 79
1.2. Service to Others and Non-Profit Groups 79
1.3. Independent Work and Initiatives 80
1.4. Connections and guidance 80
1.5. Experimentation and Individual Work 81
1.6. Learning on the Job and Accreditation 81
1.7. Gain Wisdom 82

Chapter 6: Develop Your Professional Brand and Portfolio 83
1.1. Create and maintain a network of contacts in your field 83
1.2. Make use of many online mediums 84
1.3. Participate in Group Activities 84
1.4. Find a Mentor or Mentoring Program 84
1.5. Developing Knowledge and Abilities Permanently 85
1.6. Participate in Open Source Initiatives 86
1.7. Seek Opinions and Evaluate Your Progress 86

Chapter 7: Excel in your Job Search and Interview 88
   1.1. Stand Out in the Job Market 88
      1.1.1. Making a Winning Resume and Cover Letter 88
   1.2. Strategies for Finding a Job Online 89
      1.2.1. Shine during the Interview 89
      1.2.2. Exhibiting Your Capabilities 90
   1.3. Successfully Negotiating Your Job Offer 91
      1.3.1. Communicate your needs and the reasoning 91
Chapter 8: Thrive in Your Career 93
   1.1. Embrace Lifelong Learning 93
   1.2. Attend Industry Conferences and Events 94
   1.3. Join Professional Associations and Communities 94
   1.4. Embrace Online Learning Platform 94
   1.5. Stay Abreast of Industry Trends 95
   1.6. Cultivate a Growth Mindset 96
   1.7. Build a Diverse Professional Network 96
   1.8. Stay agile and Develop problem-solving skills 97
   1.9. Seek feedback and reflect 97
   1.10. Maintain a growth mindset 98
About the Author 100
Reference 102

Introduction

The term "artificial intelligence" is used to describe the study and implementation of techniques to program computers to mimic human intellect in areas such as perception, speech recognition, decision making, and problem solving. There are concerns that as AI develops, some human-dominated occupations may be replaced by machines, resulting in fewer available jobs for people.

According to the Goldman Sachs's report on the influence of AI on the labor market, 300 million jobs could be at risk of being lost (Goldman Sachs, 2023). It's crucial to keep in mind that this is a forecast and that the actual effect on employment could be different based on a number of factors such as market conditions and government regulations. However, Goldman Sachs' estimate shows how large the impact might be and how important it is for individuals and businesses to get ready for the new AI-driven work environment.

On the contrary, AI will also create some jobs while reshaping others. However, substantial efforts to improve and retrain workers will be needed to accommodate these shifts.

This book explores the field of AI and examines its many effects on different sectors of society and businesses in an effort to help you plan and prepare for success.

In the first chapter, the stage is set by reviewing the fundamentals of AI, tracing its tremendous growth over time, and discussing the wide-ranging industries that have been affected by its disruptive innovations. In addition, I discuss the effects of AI on the labor market, ethical concerns, and economic and social repercussions.

In Chapter 2, I dig into the potential of AI in the future. Here, I explore the future of technology, various industries, and how it will affect many different fields of work, including Cybersecurity, Data Analytics, Renewable Energy, Telemedicine, and Digital Marketing. I will take a deep look at how AI is accelerating shifts in these areas, as well as the skill-sets that are essential for success now and in the coming years.

In Chapter 3, I will shift gears to encourage you to reflect on who you are as an individual, to consider your passions and skills. I offer advice on how to narrow down your interests, evaluate your skills and abilities, solicit feedback, and analyze future demands. I also explain how to make the most of market shifts, educational resources, and expert guidance in order to sustainably advance your career.

Chapter 4 prepares you to make a decision by arming you with knowledge of AI and self-evaluation. There's a focus on the value of continuing education and the importance of finding the right path to get you where you want to go in the world of AI.

In Chapter 5, I shift the focus to the importance of gaining practical experience and the resources to complement your education. I guide you toward experiences that will strengthen your practical competence through internships, mentorships, personal projects, and on-the-job training.

Chapter 6 builds on this foundation by providing guidance on creating a strong professional brand and portfolio. It stresses the value of making connections, building relationships, learning on the job, value-added contributor to project teams, and sharing one's expertise through initiatives and leadership.

In chapter 7, the focus is placed on assisting you in your job search and interviews. This involves tasks such as creating a crisp resume and cover letter, networking through social media and industry events, and making good use of digital tools. It also stresses the significance of knowing your worth and provides tactics for successfully negotiating job offers.

Last but not least, Chapter 8 is packed with advice to help you succeed in your chosen profession. It emphasizes the significance of learning new skills throughout your life, keeping abreast of technological developments, and developing resiliency and flexibility. In this chapter, I will discuss the importance of developing a growth attitude, listening to criticism, monitoring industry developments, and always striving to do better.

This book will serve as a road map to help you build a successful, future-proof career. Regardless of where you are in your professional life, the information in this book will help you better utilize the AI era to your advantage to get to the next level.

Chapter 1: Understand the Fundamentals of AI and its Implications

Artificial Intelligence (AI) has emerged as a major disruptor with the power to reshape businesses and the industries in which they operate as well as fundamentally change the way we live and work. In this chapter, we will examine some of the key aspects of AI and its effects on various aspects of our society. We will explore the capabilities of AI, the enormous changes it has the potential to bring, and the ramifications we must consider: from significant progress in a relatively short period of time to the impact on employment, the economy to ethical considerations.

1.1. *Fundamentals of AI*

In today's fast-paced, technologically-driven world, knowing the basics of artificial intelligence is no longer a luxury, rather a necessity. AI is changing the way we engage with technology and giving us the ability to reach previously unimaginable levels of efficiency and productivity, from self-driving cars to virtual assistants.

What is Artificial Intelligence?

AI is the study and creation of computer systems capable of human-level cognitive function, where machines mimic human intelligence by teaching themselves how to learn, reason, and make choices. In order these core areas, we need to explore the fascinating field of machine learning. The goal of this area of study is to develop methods for making robots capable of gaining knowledge from large datasets and improving their performance over time. Machines may learn to recognize patterns, make predictions, and adjust their actions in real time by employing algorithms and statistical models. Many applications of artificial intelligence, from voice recognition systems to recommendation engines, rely on machine learning as their backbone.

Additionally, it is important to pay special attention to deep learning, a subfield of machine learning. Deep learning models, also known as neural networks, excel in processing and interpreting complicated data because they were inspired by the human brain. These networks mimic the interconnectivity of neurons to perform tasks such as pattern recognition, image analysis, and even natural language processing. Computer vision, speech recognition, and language translation are just a few of the areas where deep learning has fueled significant advances.

In order to fully realize AI's potential, we must first fully comprehend the far-reaching effects it will have on our culture and our world. By facilitating better diagnoses, individualized treatment plans, and cutting-edge medical research, AI has the potential to completely transform the healthcare system. AI's practical applications in the business world include process automation, supply chain optimization, and improved customer service. Climate change, resource management, and disaster response are just a few examples of the global concerns that AI has the ability to help solve.

However, immense power also comes with correspondingly great responsibility. The ethical implications of AI research and development must not be ignored. Concerns about privacy, bias in algorithms, and their potential effects on the job market all deserve careful attention. To ensure openness, justice, and accountability in the design and deployment of AI systems, it is essential to encourage a responsible approach to AI development.

1.2. *Explosive Development of AI*
In recent years, we have seen exceptional growth in the field of AI, leading to major advances and innovations. This was made possible by an increase in computing power, the availability of larger sets of

data, and the refinement of machine learning algorithms, resulting in AI's rise to the forefront of innovation and practical use.

Across many fields, AI has proven its enormous potential and capabilities. The ability of AI systems to comprehend, interpret, and engage with data related to humans has improved greatly. Its capacity to understand complicated patterns and generate accurate predictions has been greatly improved by the advent of deep learning.

The widespread uses of AI in multiple industries such as healthcare, financial services, transportation, and education have also contributed to the field's meteoric rise in popularity. Organizations have recognized the immense value that AI can bring in terms of cost savings, operational efficiency, and enhanced customer experiences. This has led to massive funding for research and development, which has resulted in the ever-increasing effectiveness of AI tools.

In addition, the active AI community, which includes researchers, engineers, and entrepreneurs, has been a major factor in the development of AI by working together, sharing their expertise, and building on the discoveries of others. There has been a lot of progress made in the field thanks to open-source platforms, strong AI frameworks, and a surplus of developer tools.

There appears to be no slowdown in AI's upward trend in the near future. Deep learning, reinforcement learning, and natural language processing are all likely to continue to progress, which will lead to even greater advances in AI. The combination of AI with other disruptive technologies like the Internet of Things (IoT), Blockchain, and Robotics are also expected to spur growth in both market size and variety of use cases.

Understanding AI's extraordinary growth is vital for individuals and businesses seeking to navigate its ecosystem efficiently. By recognizing the forces driving its development and remaining informed about the newest breakthroughs, you can make informed decisions, leverage the power of AI to advance your career, build or grow your business, and contribute to defining the future of this disruptive technology.

1.3. *Disruption in Multiple Industries creating New Opportunities*

1.3.1. *Artificial Intelligence in Business*

Business operations stand to benefit greatly from AI technologies, which can make them smarter, more automated, and more data-driven. By streamlining and automating processes, improving decision-making and increasing competitiveness, businesses are enabled to do more with less.

Predictive analytics is one of the most visible use cases of AI in the corporate settings. Systems are able to sift through mountains of data in search of patterns, trends, and correlations through the use of sophisticated algorithms and machine learning techniques. This allows businesses to better predict industry trends, anticipate client needs, and proactively provide solutions.

The interaction between a business and its customers can also be greatly supported by AI. Intelligent chatbots and virtual assistants can speed up responses and boost client satisfaction with tailored, interactive service. In order to increase sales and maintain loyal customers, businesses are increasingly turning to recommendation systems powered by AI.

Furthermore, AI can help companies automate mundane jobs and improve efficiency. Automating repetitive tasks, processes and operations can help save time and eliminate room for error by using machine learning. This frees up workers' time to concentrate on more important tasks, increasing productivity and stimulating new ideas in businesses.

Additionally, AI can help businesses with risk management and fraud detection. It can evaluate massive volumes of data instantly, looking for irregularities that could signal fraud. This aids companies in reducing dangers, keeping private data secure, and guarding valuable assets.

On the contrary, adopting AI in the workplace is exciting, but not without serious risks and obstacles. There are concerns over data privacy, algorithmic unfairness, and the effects on jobs are among the most prominent ethical issues. Organizations would need to address these issues meticulously, making sure that AI systems are open, fair, and accountable.

However, in order to maintain a competitive edge in the face of AI's ongoing development, organizations must make use out of this game-changing technology for driving innovation, efficiency, and growth, whether it be through data analysis, customer engagement, or process automation.

Accenture, a leading global professional services company revealed the findings of their research of the 2019 study in a press release claiming that, "Failure to Scale Artificial Intelligence Could Put 75% of Organizations Out of Business" (Accenture, 2019). The results of the study show that many companies are not properly scaling their AI programs, which could have disastrous effects. The study found that if companies don't properly grow their AI efforts, 75% of them risk being left behind or going out of business.

In order to fully reap AI's benefits and secure its long-term viability, the paper stresses the need to scale it across a company. It stresses the need of companies coordinating their AI plans with their overarching company goals and creating a detailed road map for rollout.

A major takeaway from the research is the need for an integrated strategy that accounts for not only AI but also data, talent, and organizational culture in order to scale effectively. It stresses the importance of firms making investments in AI capabilities, such as data infrastructure, talent acquisition and development, and an atmosphere that encourages experimentation and innovation.

Data quality and availability, integration with existing systems, and assuring ethical and responsible AI practices are just a few of the obstacles highlighted in the report as firms try to scale their AI programs. This shows how crucial it is to find solutions to these problems if we are to fully realize AI's promise and use it to our advantage in the marketplace.

1.3.2. *Artificial Intelligence in Healthcare*

AI has the potential to advance medical diagnostics and enhance the accuracy of disease detection. For example, by analyzing X-rays, MRIs, and CT scans, machine learning algorithms can help radiologists make more precise diagnoses. Algorithms driven by AI can swiftly scan massive amounts of medical data, allowing doctors to see patterns and make better decisions regarding patient treatment.

In addition, AI can be a crucial component of individualized healthcare and treatment strategy. Medical records, genetic information, and patient lifestyle characteristics can all be analyzed with the use of AI algorithms, allowing for more individualized care. By analyzing a patient's unique traits, AI can help determine the optimal medicine, dosage, and treatment plan to maximize positive outcomes while minimizing unwanted side effects.

Chatbots and digital medical assistants are also being developed with the help of AI. These AI-driven apps can have meaningful conversations with patients, answer their questions, and give them basic medical guidance. The use of Virtual Assistants can increase patient involvement and self-care by facilitating monitoring of health problems, medication adherence reminders, and access to real-time health insights.

1.3.3. *Artificial Intelligence in Pharmaceutical*

Similarly, AI is leading progress in the realms of pharmaceutical research and development. Potential drug candidates and their efficacy can be identified and predicted using machine learning algorithms by analyzing massive volumes of biomedical data such as research papers, clinical trial data, and patient information. By optimizing trial designs and locating appropriate patient populations, AI can accelerate the development of new therapies and their delivery to patients.

On the other hand, there are obstacles to implementing AI in the healthcare and pharmaceutical industries. Confidentiality and trust in the healthcare system depends on resolving issues including data privacy, security, and ethics.

1.3.4. *Artificial Intelligence in the Financial Services Industry*

AI is having a significant impact on the financial services industry as well, particularly in the areas of data analysis and decision making. AI systems can deliver important insights and predictive analytics by processing massive volumes of financial data in real time. They can evaluate market trends, client behavior, and financial patterns to find profitable trading opportunities, improve portfolio management, and increase returns.

Additionally, AI is improving financial risk management. Data anomalies and trends are easy targets for machine learning algorithms, which makes them useful for spotting fraud and other threats. Real-time monitoring of transactions can allow for the identification of potentially fraudulent activities. This can help financial services organizations meet regulatory requirements and enhance the security of financial transactions.

The fields of customer service and personal financial management are also seeing significant advancements. AI-enabled Chatbots and Virtual Assistants can help customers with their finances by answering frequently asked questions, facilitating transactions, and offering individualized advice. Customers can have better experiences and be more engaged with financial institutions if AI algorithms examine their data and preferences to offer more personalized products and services.

Similarly, algorithmic trading and quantitative finance are two other areas where AI can make a significant impact. AI systems can quickly and accurately evaluate massive amounts of market data, spot patterns, and place trades. These can result in higher profits, faster.

However, there are risks associated with using AI in the financial sector such as ethical problems, privacy issues, and algorithmic biases. In order to make sure AI is used responsibly and keep customers' best interests in mind, we need regulations and monitoring.

1.3.5. *Artificial Intelligence in Transportation*

The creation of fully autonomous vehicles is a prime example of how AI is revolutionizing the transportation industry. Self-driving cars, trucks, and other vehicles are made possible with the help of algorithms and machine learning techniques. These automated systems can safely move through their environments without any human intervention due to their ability to sense their context utilizing a variety of sensors and make judgments in real time. The widespread adoption of autonomous cars has the potential to drastically improve public transportation.

Transportation networks are also being optimized with the help of AI-powered traffic management technologies. In order to better manage traffic flow, congestion, and signal timing, systems can examine data from sensors, cameras, and connected vehicles in real time. Travel times can be shortened, road capacity increased, and transportation efficiency boosted because of its ability to automatically alter traffic signals and provide drivers with real-time traffic information.

Furthermore, AI can improve productivity and streamlining processes in the logistics and supply chain sector. Freight routing, scheduling, and distribution can be optimized using algorithms, resulting in savings and faster delivery times. In addition, through the help of machine learning models' analysis of historical data, the system can predict demand trends, improve inventory management, and cut down on supply chain inefficiencies.

Smart transportation systems are also being built. Surveillance systems driven by AI, for instance, can keep tabs on traffic, spot problems, and notify authorities immediately. Public transit, ridesharing, and bike-sharing are just a few examples of how public transportation may be improved.

1.3.6. *Artificial Intelligence in Education*

AI is having a considerable effect in education, particularly in the realm of individualized instruction. The learning habits, interests, and academic performance of each individual student can be evaluated via learning platforms and intelligent tutoring systems. It can increase learning results and student engagement by tailoring content, pace, and difficulty to each individual student's needs.

Educational resources such as articles, films, or interactive materials can be recommended to students based on their interests, learning styles, and knowledge gaps through intelligent content recommendation systems. This encourages students to take charge of their own education and broaden their horizons by providing them with access to a wealth of resources for learning on their own time and at their pace.

Automated grading and feedback systems are another way that AI can be used in the classroom. Students' work can be graded by algorithms in real time, with immediate feedback on their strengths and areas for growth. As a result, Teachers' workloads are lightened, feedback loops are shortened, and timely guidance and support are provided to students.

In addition, virtual assistants or chatbots can be created to help with administrative duties, answer questions, and give 24/7 support to both students and educators. These AI-enabled Assistants can field basic questions, allowing teachers more time for one-on-one instruction.

AI is also making it easier to analyze massive amounts of data, such as student grades, attendance records, and learning analytics. Educators and institutions can use data mining and machine learning approaches to quickly sort through this mountain of data in search of patterns and insights that will lead to better teaching and learning practices.

1.4. *Implications and Challenges*

1.4.1. *Impact on the Job Market*

The rise of AI has far-reaching repercussions for employment and the economy. Although many jobs may be lost to automation, others would be created, and some will be reshaped. In order to thrive in this era, individuals will need to learn new skills and commit to continuous learning, while policymakers will need to devise plans to make the transition as smooth and equitable as possible for everyone.

AI will change the set of talents employers seek in prospective employees, resulting in elimination of jobs requiring repetitive tasks. By relieving people of these duties, automation will free them up to focus on more challenging and creative jobs in areas such as data science, machine learning, AI engineering, and ethical governance to support the creation, deployment, and upkeep of systems.

Furthermore, some occupations may change, instead of being completely eliminated. By combining human and AI resources, workers can make better decisions and work more efficiently. AI-powered products and services, for instance, can aid medical professionals in making diagnoses and aid customer service agents in making tailored suggestions.

As a result of this shift, workers will need to acquire new abilities and adjust to working alongside AI systems. It is essential that they participate in re-skilling and up-skilling programs. In a labor market increasingly dominated by AI, keeping one's skills current and relevant through lifelong learning is crucial.

Additionally, the social and economic effects of AI on the labor market are substantial and must be considered. If some portions of the workforce are left behind or do not have access to re-skilling opportunities, income inequality could rise. Inclusionary policies, equal opportunities in education and training, and strong social safety nets are all necessary to close these gaps. Individuals and businesses should prepare themselves for the shifting job market and capture opportunities by anticipating the effects of AI.

1.4.2. *Ethical Considerations*

Further advancement in AI and its use will be fundamentally influenced by ethical considerations. In order to adopt AI in a responsible and ethical manner, we should address issues of prejudice, fairness, protect privacy, promote transparency, guarantee safety, and think about the social and economic consequences.

It is imperative to note that in terms fairness, AI systems are only as objective as the information they are taught to make decisions with. Unfair results or discrimination may result if the data's inherent biases are not addressed through transparent and responsible system design and training to remove prejudice from data collecting, algorithm design, and decision making.

AI requires massive volumes of data for training and enhancing its performance, which raises concerns about privacy and data protection. Data privacy and security are at risk because of this. Data collection and use should be subject to informed consent, and sensitive data should be protected through the use of secure procedures.

Security and safety should be top priorities for AI systems with real-world applications like driverless automobiles and industrial robots. Systems should be designed with strict safety precautions, in line with industry standards, and address potential dangers and vulnerabilities.

The primary purpose of AI should be to improve the lives of humans, uphold society ideals, and expand human potential. Systems should be made this in mind, accountable and subject to human oversight so that they can best serve human needs and advance society. This necessitates stringent governance frameworks and legislation. Ethical norms, standards, and regulatory structures can only be developed by joint efforts of governments, institutions, and interested parties. This ensures the ethical and transparent advancement and application of AI.

In short, we can maximize AI's positive effects while limiting its negative ones, and create a society that is led by AI in a way that is fair and inclusive, and ultimately improve people's lives.

Chapter 2: Discover and Embrace the Future of AI

As the job market continues to evolve, there are several main sectors where future career and business possibilities are projected to emerge. Thriving in this shifting market demands a combination of technical skills, adaptability, and a commitment to constant learning. In this chapter, I will cover several major areas where future career possibilities are projected to develop and highlight the skills needed to thrive in these roles.

1.1. *AI Advancements causing Global Disruption*

Global markets are being disrupted by AI and only people that are open to new ideas and willing to make an impact will do well in the jobs and businesses of the future. Envision yourself as a cutting-edge AI engineer working to create intelligent systems that improve our everyday lives or an Entrepreneur creating new and convenient ways to do deliver value to customers. Try to put yourself in the shoes of a machine learning expert, someone who uses data to uncover insights that drive decision making and improve efficiency. Consider, instead, the work of a data scientist, whose job it is to sift through mountains of data in search of elusive patterns that can inform strategic decisions. Technicians and specialists experienced in developing, programming, and maintaining automated systems will be important as robotics and automation gain traction. Those that are open to new technologies and the possibilities they present have a bright future ahead of them.

1.2. *High Demand Careers and Businesses of the Future*

1.2.1. *Cybersecurity*

The importance of strong Cybersecurity will skyrocket in the AI era, with its ever-changing digital landscape. There is a growing need for trained personnel who can safeguard sensitive information and guarantee the security of digital infrastructure as a result of the proliferation of new cyber dangers made possible by the widespread adoption of AI across several industries. Cybersecurity experts will be increasingly important to protect private data and ensure the safety of the digital infrastructure that supports our globalized society as AI continues to influence the future.

There has been a significant shift in the nature of cyber dangers in the modern AI era. Cyberattacks are becoming more complex in tandem with the development of AI technology. The use of algorithms by bad actors to create more precise and versatile attack methods has reduced the efficacy of conventional security measures. Cybersecurity experts in today's environment need to be nimble enough to anticipate new attacks and adapt their defenses accordingly using artificial intelligence.

AI provides potent tools for enhancing Cybersecurity in the face of complex and ever-evolving cyber threats. Machine learning algorithms can examine large databases for abnormalities, patterns, and security holes. Continuous network monitoring, anomalous activity detection and immediate alerts to security personnel are all possible with AI-powered threat detection solutions. Moreover, AI-driven behavioral analytics may evaluate user conduct to identify security breaches. These AI-driven tools permit early detection and mitigation of risks, as well as proactive defense against them.

Roles in Cybersecurity
The need for trained Cybersecurity experts is only expected to increase as the AI revolution progresses. There has been a rise in need for specialists in areas like artificial intelligence security architecture, data privacy analysis, and threat intelligence analysis in the field of Cybersecurity. Experts like these are a necessity for businesses to meet the stringent requirements of the industry in which they operate.

Here are key roles in Cybersecurity and what they do:

- *Security Analyst:* Monitor system security and analyze events and create countermeasures. They research security flaws and suggest fixes to fix them.
- *Ethical Hacker / Penetration Tester:* Probe computer and network defenses for flaws. Their job is to discover security flaws before they may be exploited by hackers.
- *Security Engineer:* Create, develop, and deploy safe systems and infrastructure. They create safeguards against cyber attacks; include security protocols, firewall settings, and IDS management.
- *Incident Responder:* Responsible for handling security incidents. They find out what happened, how bad it was, how to fix it, and how to prevent it from happening again.
- *Security Architect:* Design and implement organizational security systems and frameworks, protect the privacy of users' information, the team creates policies, evaluates potential threats, and designs safe networks and infrastructure.
- *Cryptographer:* Ensure the safety of sensitive information and communications by designing, testing, and implementing various cryptographic methods and protocols. They create secure communication protocols and devise new forms of encryption.

- *Security Consultant:* Advise on security and make recommendations based on extensive experience. They analyze threats, create protection plans, and advise businesses on how to strengthen their security measures.
- *Compliance Officer:* Ensure conformity with all applicable security legislation and guidelines. Conduct audits, create policies for security, and check that all necessary safeguards are in place.

To learn more about their specific requirements, use a search engine to look up desired job titles. Make use of social networking sites such as Linkedin geared at professionals, as well as company-specific career pages. Look at the job advertisements, making sure you have the relevant credentials, abilities, certifications, and education.

Factors for Success

Individuals will need to have knowledge and skills in the following areas:
- Cybersecurity frameworks and certifications such as CompTIA Security+, CEH, and CISSP
- Knowledge and experience in encryption protocols and safe coding standards;
- AI algorithms, machine learning, and data analysis; and

- Soft skills such as critical thinking, problem solving, and good communication will be essential for working in multidisciplinary teams and recognizing new security risks.

Future Prospects

The importance of Cybersecurity experts will continue to grow as the AI continues to develop. There are advantages and disadvantages to its rapid development. While it has the potential to greatly improve measures, AI also presents new opportunities for cybercriminals. Professionals in the field need to be aware of new dangers and should focus on constantly learning to improve their knowledge and abilities to keep up with the latest trends.

1.2.2. *Data Analysis and Science*

AI has allowed big data to expand rapidly at an unprecedented scale and it will take the skills of Data Analysts and Scientists to fully realize its potential. By processing and analyzing large datasets, AI systems can reveal previously unknown patterns, correlations, and trends, which will provide businesses competitive advantages in areas such as decision making, product development, and market expansion. The capacity to glean useful information from large datasets is more important than ever for businesses that want to stay ahead of the competition.

Roles in Data Analysis and Science

The rise of AI has resulted in a surge for qualified Data Analysts and Scientists. The work of Data Analysts is crucial in the transformation of raw data into useful information. Their function goes beyond the scope of conventional data analysis. Here what is Data Analysts do:

- Collect, cleanse, analyze, and interpret massive datasets required for decision-making through AI-powered tools and algorithms to make sense of large datasets, spot trends, and draw useful conclusions;
- Work with different departments to learn about the company's goals, develop research questions, and create trials that will yield useful information; and
- Use of their communication skills to help stakeholders make informed decisions based on collected data.

Similarly, here is what Data Scientists do:

- Use their superior analytical and programming skills to examine large datasets, create cutting-edge machine learning models, and then deliver actionable insights and forecasts that help businesses make better decisions;
- Collaborate with business leaders to define challenges, ask questions that may be answered with data, and develop

algorithms to mine massive databases for useful information; and
- Help businesses improve efficiency, individualize customer service, and unleash creativity.

Note: To learn more about their specific requirements, use a search engine to look up desired job titles.

Factors for Success

To succeed in data analysis and science positions in the age of AI, you need a unique set of abilities, including technical know-how, subject experience, and a need for lifelong learning and professional development. Here is an example of some required and preferred qualifications (to learn more about their specific requirements, use a search engine to look up desired job titles):

- Knowledge of statistics, programming (preferably in Python or R), and machine learning methods is required;
- Data Analysts and Scientists will also need to keep up with the latest developments in AI software and hardware;
- Understanding the setting in which data is obtained and correctly interpreting the results will require in-depth domain expertise; and
- Excellent communication to effectively collaborate with stakeholders and create organizational impact.

Future Prospects

It will be a golden age for Data Analysts and Scientists. These experts will have the knowledge to unlock the potential of massive datasets, revealing crucial insights that guide tactical and strategic decision-making. The need for qualified data analysis and scientific workers is expected to skyrocket as AI continues to develop and grow.

Simultaneously, ethical concerns will continue to become more pressing as data analysis and research advance. Data privacy, security, and transparency must be top priorities for experts in these domains. The reliability and social impact of data-driven judgments depend on safeguarding their usage of AI and preventing its misuse.

1.2.3. Renewable Energy

To battle climate change and establish a sustainable future, the world is embracing renewable energy sources at an unprecedented pace. Jobs and businesses in renewable energy are emerging as catalysts for change, transforming the energy sector. When applied to renewable energy systems, AI has the potential to increase efficiency, strengthen dependability, and hasten the worldwide shift to clean power.

Solar, wind, and hydroelectric power are all examples of renewable energy that will be essential to society in the years to come. AI will greatly improve the effectiveness and efficiency of renewable energy systems through algorithms that can optimize energy production and implement predictive maintenance. The accuracy of forecasts will be enhanced by machine learning algorithms, allowing for more efficient use of renewable energy sources. In addition, demand response management will be made easier by algorithms, which help keep energy supply and demand in equilibrium in real time. The combination of AI and renewable energy holds great potential for accelerating progress toward the goal of universalizing high-quality, affordable clean energy.

Roles in Renewable Energy

Incredible expansion in the renewable energy industry will open up a wide range of new professional possibilities. Individuals that are well-versed in both AI and renewable energy systems will be in great demand as the sector adapts to realize the full potential of AI in the renewable energy space. These experts can create and improve systems, maximize the use of renewable energy sources, and ensure effective use of all available materials. Here are the different roles and what they do:
- *Energy Optimization Analyst:* Responsible for evaluating energy consumption and coming up with ways to improve

efficiency, cut expenses, and lessen negative effects on the environment;

- *Data Scientist:* Gather, analyze, and interpret large data sets in order to draw conclusions, make decisions, and create new approaches to problems that face businesses using their analytical and programming skills;
- *AI Integration Specialist*: Responsible for providing a seamless integration between AI systems with other technologies for optimal productivity;
- *Sustainability Expert*: Promote corporate environmental and social responsibility, the adoption of eco-friendly procedures, and the creation of plans to reduce negative effects on the environment caused by business activities;
- *Project Manager*: Manage and organize all facets of a project, from its inception to its completion; and
- *Policy Analyst*: Conduct research, analyze data, and assess policy to draw conclusions and provide suggestions to government, non-profit, or private business.

Note: To learn more about their specific requirements, use a search engine to look up desired job titles

Factors for Success

The ability to plan, construct, and maintain solar, wind, or hydropower systems will be essential for professionals in this field. Here is an example of some required and preferred qualifications:

- Expertise in renewable energy systems, AI technology, and sustainability will all be necessary for success; and
- Knowledge of programming languages and experience with data visualization tools will also be quite helpful when sifting through massive volumes of energy data.

Future Prospects

Experts in the field of renewable energy will have a significant impact on the trajectory of humanity's energy future. Reducing greenhouse gas emissions and adapting to a changing climate requires widespread use of renewable energy. These experts can make renewable energy systems more effective, reliable, and financially viable by utilizing AI technologies. Their efforts will help advance goals of energy autonomy, ecological protection, and green employment creation. Furthermore, they play a crucial role in creating novel solutions, shedding light on renewable energy regulations, and propelling the worldwide shift towards sustainable energy ecology.

While there is great potential in using AI for renewable energy, there are also significant obstacles to overcome. It is critical to ensure ethical AI techniques and address data privacy and security concerns. Industry, governments, and academics must work together to design regulatory frameworks, stimulate research and development, and encourage the responsible deployment of AI in renewable energy systems.

1.2.4. *Augmented and Virtual Reality (VR/AR)*

There is no limit to what can be accomplished with technologies like VR and AR revolutionizing our experience of digital media. Fascinating new job opportunities will emerge at the intersection of virtual reality, augmented reality, and artificial intelligence, which will revolutionize every sector, from the gaming industry to the manufacturing sector.

Algorithms powered by AI will improve the realism and interactivity of virtual and augmented reality experiences, making them more immersive. Using machine learning, we can improve AR overlays and provide individualized user experiences in real time. Voice commands made possible by natural language processing will improve the usability of these systems. Applications ranging from medical diagnostics and architectural design to training simulations and virtual collaboration can benefit greatly from the combination of AI and VR/AR technology.

Experts in VR and AR are pioneering the development of cutting-edge media. Gaming, entertainment, education, healthcare, and engineering are just few of the fields that could benefit greatly from these technologies. Experts may utilize AI to design lifelike simulations and digital learning spaces that can be customized to each individual user. Virtual reality and augmented reality allow for remote teamwork, travel without leaving home, and interactive storytelling, all of which pave the way for new forms of expression and invention. The work of these experts is essential to the establishment of norms, the expansion of technical capabilities, and the revolution in user engagement with digital media.

Types of Roles in VR and AR

The VR and AR sectors are booming, creating numerous job openings such as VR and AR Developer, AI Integrator, Content Creator, and User Experience Designer. Here are the different roles and what they do:

- Engineers and Developers: Create lifelike environments and interactive features by incorporating AI algorithms through the development of exciting images and dynamic settings.

- Designers and Content Creators: Specialize in user experience and interface make sure users of VR and AR apps have a pleasant time.
- Data Scientists and AI experts: Improve VR and AR systems by expanding AI-driven features and enhancing tailored suggestions.

Note: To learn more about their specific requirements, use a search engine to look up desired job titles.

Factors for Success

It takes a unique blend of technical know-how, creative thinking, and agility to succeed in the VR and AR careers.

Here is an example of some required and preferred qualifications:

- Experience with development platforms like Unity or Unreal Engine is a must;
- AI skills to incorporate capabilities such as machine learning algorithms and computer vision into VR and AR experiences;
- Knowledge in programming languages such as C#, Python, or JavaScript is essential for creating such dynamic software;
- Creativity and design skills to create visually compelling and engaging experiences; and

- Excellent communication and collaboration abilities are required to work with interdisciplinary.

Future Prospects

The convergence of VR, AR, and AI is expected to grow and bring about radical changes in business and a wealth of new opportunities for skilled workers. Experts in VR and AR are crucial to the development of future interactive digital experiences. These experts can redefine how we study, play, and interact with the digital world by combining their technical knowledge, imagination, and ability to work together.

There are still obstacles to VR and AR. Improvements in realism and the ability to create seamless experiences require developments in AI algorithms, hardware capabilities, and data processing. Privacy of user information, use of AI in a responsible manner, and ease of access are also important factors to think about. To overcome these obstacles and ensure the ethical adoption of AI-driven VR and AR technologies, a concerted effort from the private sector, the academic community, and governments is required. Progress in AI, VR, and AR holds great promise for the future by expanding our horizons and changing the way we experience and engage with digital media.

1.2.5. *Telemedicine and Healthcare*

The widespread adoption of AI technologies is propelling the healthcare sector towards revolutionary change. AI solutions are opening the doors for ambitious individuals who want to use technology to make a positive impact in the world. From patient care, to accessibility, and efficiency; will all see a major boosts as a result of these changes.

Today's medical practitioners can take advantage of cutting-edge AI-powered diagnosis and treatment technologies. In order to aid in the early detection of diseases, precise diagnosis, and individualized treatment regimens, AI diagnostic systems can evaluate massive amounts of medical data. With the help of machine learning algorithms, Radiologists can better detect anomalies in medical images by spotting patterns and trends. AI powered decision support systems provide clinicians with evidence-based therapy suggestions. These developments increase the standard of care provided to patients, lead to better health outcomes, and make medical operations more efficient.

Similarly, in healthcare analytics, data analytics and AI are causing major change. Data analysts and Scientists in the healthcare industry are indispensable for sifting through mountains of patient information in search of patterns and insights. Professionals in these fields can use AI algorithms to better manage populations, allocate resources, and prevent disease. With the use of AI predictive analytics, healthcare providers can better prepare for and respond to disease outbreaks. In addition, clinical documentation is improved by AI-enabled natural language processing, leading to higher levels of precision, productivity, and patient safety.

Roles in Remote Healthcare and Telemedicine

Furthermore, the use of AI has enabled a dramatic shift towards telemedicine in the medical field. Jobs in telemedicine include a wide spectrum, from telemedicine professionals to analysts of medical data to remote healthcare providers. Here are the different roles and what they do:

- *Telehealth Providers:* Medical experts such as doctors, nurses, and medical specialists, who use the internet to conduct in-depth patient evaluations, make diagnoses, and outline treatment strategies;
- *Telehealth Coordinators:* Oversee the organizational and operational facets of providing healthcare via electronic means. Appointments are scheduled, virtual visits are coordinated, new patients are registered, and electronic health records are maintained.

- *Information Technology (IT) Data Security Specialists*: Play an essential role in protecting the confidentiality of patients' personal information in the telemedicine industry. They set up strict safety protocols, keep their networks protected, and fix any technical problems that crop up.
- *Telemedicine Technicians:* Help get systems up and running for remote medical care so that patients and doctors can communicate efficiently.
- *Remote Patient Monitoring Specialist:* Collect and examine medical data and patient vitals from a distance. They collaborate closely with other members of the medical staff to monitor patients and take corrective action as needed.
- *Telepharmacist:* Pharmacist who works remotely and communicates with patients through the internet to study medical records, check prescriptions, and give advice on medications. They are essential to the provision of safe and efficient medication administration in outlying healthcare facilities.
- Telehealth Educators: Teach doctors and patients about the advantages of telemedicine. They aid in making sure that everyone can make good use of remote healthcare technologies.

All of these functions work together to make telemedicine and remote healthcare more accessible, more convenient, and more effective for patients in far-flung areas. These professionals use AI systems to deliver medical advice across vast distances, confer with patients virtually, and keep tabs on their health from afar. With the help of AI algorithms, we can analyze patient data in real time and provide better, more preventative care. Telemedicine has many benefits, including increased efficiency, decreased costs, and a more convenient experience for patients, especially in underserved areas.

Factors for Success

It takes a special combination of skills that blends medical knowledge with AI understanding to succeed in healthcare and telemedicine careers in the age of AI. Here is an example of some required and preferred qualifications:

- Medical workers need extensive knowledge in medicine, disease, and patient care along with an educational degree, experience, and license or certification depending on the role.
- Effective use of AI technologies requires knowledge of AI algorithms, machine learning, and data analysis methods.
- Requires programming language skills, such as Python or R.

- Soft skills: Effective communication, empathy, and the capacity to create trust with patients.

Note: To learn more about specific requirements, use a search engine to look up desired job titles.

Future Prospects

Opportunities abound for tech-savvy medical professionals who are committed to using AI to advance healthcare and telemedicine. Jobs in telemedicine are facilitating the delivery of healthcare to geographically dispersed populations. In order to extract insights and drive evidence-based decision making, healthcare data analysts and scientists are making use of AI-enabled analytics. As a result, a more accessible, efficient, and patient-centric healthcare ecosystem will be developed as the AI advances due to continued collaboration, ethical considerations, and continual learning.

When it comes to healthcare and telemedicine, ethics must take center stage. Protecting patient confidentiality, keeping data secure, and using AI ethically are all priorities. Establishing ethical principles and laws requires close cooperation between healthcare practitioners, AI researchers, lawmakers, and regulatory organizations. To keep up with the ever-changing landscape of AI technologies in healthcare, continual research, development, and continuous learning are essential.

1.2.6. *E-commerce and Digital Marketing*

Business-to-consumer interactions and product sales have been completely transformed by the advent of e-commerce and digital marketing in the age of artificial intelligence. The incorporation of AI technology into the digital world is influencing the future of e-commerce and digital marketing. Algorithms, machine learning, and data analytics powered by artificial intelligence are helping businesses improve their interactions with customers, develop more targeted marketing campaigns, and increase revenue. This article examines the state of e-commerce and digital marketing employment in the age of artificial intelligence, focusing on their revolutionary potential, necessary skills, and crucial role in determining the course of online business.

The use of AI is revolutionizing how e-commerce companies can provide a unique shopping experience for each individual customer. Artificial intelligence systems sift through mountains of data about customers' online activities, purchases, and demographics. This information is used to provide customers tailored product suggestions, marketing messages, and deals. Chatbots and virtual assistants powered by AI help businesses better serve their customers by resolving their issues and questions immediately. Incorporating AI into online retail improves the shopping experience for customers, encourages more interaction, and drives up conversions.

Digital marketing techniques have been completely transformed by the use of data analytics and AI algorithms. In the marketing world, AI-powered solutions allow for the study of consumer habits, the detection of trends, and the forecasting of tastes. This data-driven strategy helps firms zero in on desirable clientele, fine-tune their advertising efforts, and distribute their resources efficiently. Content production tools powered by AI make it easy to cater to customers' unique tastes and interests. What is more, artificial intelligence-driven predictive analytics aids marketers in predicting industry trends, making educated judgments, and maximizing ROI.

The advent of AI has resulted in a proliferation of positions in the digital marketing and e-commerce industries. Experts in areas such as digital marketing, artificial intelligence algorithms, data analytics, and e-commerce platforms are in high demand. Managers in the e-commerce sector are in charge of running online stores, making sure customers have a positive experience, and implementing AI-powered solutions to increase sales. To better target customers and boost the effectiveness of marketing campaigns, data analysts and scientists glean insights from customer data, conduct market research, and create AI models.

Advertising campaigns, customer engagement, and conversion rates can all be improved with the help of AI-powered tools and data used by digital marketers. Designers specializing in user experience and interface (UX/UI) work to improve the usability of e-commerce sites for consumers.

Roles in Digital Marketing and Ecommerce

Professionals who are interested in utilizing data and technology to promote business success have a great deal to gain from the widespread adoption of AI technologies in e-commerce and digital marketing. Here are the different roles and what they do:

- *Digital Marketing Manager:* Create and implement a digital marketing plan to boost website visits, brand recognition, and sales leads.
- *Social Media Strategist:* Create and execute social media strategy development and implementation for increased brand awareness, participation from key demographics, and action from your target audience.
- *SEO Specialist:* Optimize search engines, website, and content to the top of search engine result pages and attract targeted visitors without paying for advertising.
- *Content Marketer:* Produce and disseminate high-quality content across many digital channels to reach and engage your intended audience.

- *Ecommerce Manager:* Manage and maintain an online store to ensure it is running efficiently and effectively.
- *Conversion Rate Optimizer:* Assess the site's current state to determine areas for enhancement to boost conversion rates.

Note: To learn more about specific requirements, use a search engine to look up desired job titles.

Professionals in digital marketing and e-commerce are well-versed in AI are at the forefront of improving the consumer experience, honing marketing techniques, and increasing revenue. To ensure that businesses can leverage the power of AI to create personalized experiences and build enduring consumer relationships in the digital world, teamwork, ethical considerations, and constant learning will shape the future of e-commerce and digital marketing.

Factors for Success

In the age of artificial intelligence, success in the fields of e-commerce and digital marketing calls on a unique blend of technological know-how, originality, and insight into customer preferences. Knowledge of online marketplaces, web analytics software, and AI algorithms is needed. Effective marketing plans require data analysis skills, particularly:

- Strong competency in Search Engine Optimization (SEO), Search Engine Marketing (SEM), and Social Media Marketing (SMM);
- Ability to draw conclusions from customer data;
- Create captivating content that resonates with customers with their creativity and storytelling skills; and
- Soft skill: Excellent communication and teamwork abilities.

Future Prospects

The demand of Digital Marketing and Ecommerce will continue to grow. However, ethical concerns will continue to reshape the e-commerce and digital marketing sector. Protection of personal information, openness, and ethical use of AI are all essential. Establishing ethical principles and rules requires cooperation between corporations, industry organizations, and legislators. To preserve customer confidence and guarantee the proper application of AI technology in e-commerce and digital marketing, ongoing study of these areas is required.

In a nutshell, developments in technology, concerns about the environment, and shifting social demands will determine the nature of work in the future. To make the most of them, you will need to be proactive in building your abilities, learning new things, and being flexible. Future professionals should train their minds to think critically, creatively, and collaboratively in addition to honing their technical skills and expanding their knowledge of emerging subjects. Individuals can best prepare themselves for the dynamic and fascinating jobs of the future by being informed, remaining nimble, and embracing lifelong learning.

Chapter 3: Evaluate Your Interests and Strengths

As you assess your interests, think about the types of problems you enjoy solving or the technologies that fascinate you the most. Do you enjoy architecting technical solutions or are you more intrigued by the intricacies of securing computer networks? In this chapter, we will explore the importance of understanding your passions and aligning them to your future career path to make sure that you derive satisfaction and fulfillment from your work.

Alongside assessing your interests, it's essential to evaluate your existing skills and knowledge related to IT. Consider the technical skills you may have acquired through different sources such as formal training, education, work experience, or personal projects. Start by assessing your proficiency in diverse areas of IT such as blockchain, IOT, cloud, software applications, mobile, databases, etc. Identify the areas where you feel confident and competent.

Simultaneously, recognize the areas where you may need further development. Pinpoint any gaps in your knowledge or skills that may be hindering your progress. This could involve learning a new programming language, gaining expertise in cloud computing, or enhancing your understanding of data analysis techniques. Acknowledging these areas for improvement would provide an opportunity for growth.

It is imperative to consider seeking feedback from mentors, instructors or professionals in the field who can provide insights into your strengths and areas of improvement. Their perspectives can help you gain a more comprehensive understanding of your skills and potential directions for growth.

Furthermore, by assessing your interests and skills, you lay a solid foundation for your journey. This self-reflection and evaluation process will help you make informed decisions about the specific career path or business you want to pursue. It will enable you to choose the right specialization that aligns with your passions and strengths.

Moreover, assessing your interests and skills will guide your decisions regarding education and training. It helps you identify the areas where you need to acquire additional knowledge or develop new abilities. Whether through pursuing a degree, earning an industry or technology specific certification, enrolling in specialized courses, or participating in practical projects; this self-assessment will guide your choices and ensure that you are on a path towards continual improvement and success.

Remember, technology is vast and rapidly evolving, so it's crucial to regularly reassess your interests and skills. As you gain more experience and explore new technologies, your passions and strengths may evolve. Embrace a growth mindset, be open to learning, and continuously assess and adapt your interests and skills to stay at the forefront of the ever-changing IT landscape.

1.1. *Identify Your Passion and Interest within IT*

A successful career is built on a strong foundation of passion and interest in the field. To truly thrive and find fulfillment, it's crucial to identify the areas within the field that ignite your enthusiasm and drive your curiosity.

1.1.1. *Explore Different Specializations*

Take the time to dig into various specializations available within the IT sector. Each area offers unique challenges, opportunities, and areas of focus. Research the responsibilities and key skills associated with roles such as software development, cybersecurity, data analysis, network administration, artificial intelligence, or user experience design. Consider the type of work involved, the problems you would be solving, and the impact you could make in each area. This exploration will help you narrow down your options and identify the specific domains that align with your interests.

1.1.2. *Reflect on Your Skills and Aptitudes*

Evaluate your existing skills and aptitudes to identify your natural strengths within the IT field. Think about the technical skills you have acquired through education, work experience, or personal projects. Assess your ability to understand complex systems, solve problems logically, and adapt to new technologies. Reflect on any feedback you have received regarding your performance in IT-related tasks.

By recognizing your innate abilities, you can focus on areas where you have a natural aptitude and enjoy working.

1.1.3. *Consider Personal Interests*

Take into account your personal interests and hobbies outside of technology. Reflect on the activities that bring you joy and fulfillment. Consider how these interests can intersect with different IT specializations. For instance, if you have a passion for design, user experience design or front-end development might be a natural fit. If you enjoy analyzing data or working with numbers, data analysis or business intelligence could be an exciting path to explore. By aligning your personal passions with IT, you can find a career that resonates with your unique interests and allows you to integrate your hobbies into your professional journey.

1.1.4. *Seek Experiences and Exposure*

Engage yourself in IT by seeking out hands-on experiences and exposure to different domains. Engage in online tutorials, certification preparation training, specialized courses, or workshops to gain practical skills and a deeper understanding of various IT disciplines. Participate in coding challenges or open-source projects to collaborate with like-minded individuals and expand your knowledge. Actively seek internships, part-time positions, or volunteer opportunities in areas that align with your potential career interests. These experiences will provide valuable insights into the day-to-day work, challenges, and rewards associated with different IT roles. They will also help you assess your level of interest, engagement, and aptitude in specific domains.

By identifying your passion and interest within the IT field, you lay the foundation for a rewarding and purpose-driven career. Passion is what fuels your motivation to learn, grow, and excel in your chosen specialization. It will prepare you to embrace challenges, persist through obstacles, and continuously adapt to the ever-evolving world of technology. Remember, your passion and interest are unique to you, so embrace the journey of self-discovery and explore the vast opportunities within the IT field to find a career path that aligns with your authentic self.

1.2. *Technical Skills Assessment:*

Start by conducting a comprehensive assessment of your technical skills. Consider the programming languages, databases, operating systems, and other technologies you are familiar with. Reflect on your experience in developing software applications, configuring networks, troubleshooting hardware or software issues, or managing databases. Make a list of the technical skills you possess, categorizing them based on proficiency levels (e.g., beginner, intermediate, advanced). This evaluation will help you identify your areas of expertise and expertise gaps that you may need to address.

1.3. *Education and Training*

Reflect on your education and any IT-related training you have received. Consider the courses, certifications, or level of education you have completed. Assess how these academic experiences have equipped you with the necessary knowledge and skills for your desired IT career path. Identify areas where you may need further education or specialized training to enhance your expertise.

1.4. *Practical Experience:*

Evaluate the practical experience you have gained in IT. This includes any internships, part-time jobs, volunteer work or projects where you applied your IT skills. Reflect on the responsibilities you had, the challenges you faced, and the outcomes you achieved. Consider the feedback you received from supervisors or colleagues regarding your performance. Assess how these practical experiences have contributed to your growth and development in the IT field.

1.5. *Seek Feedback:*

Don't hesitate to seek feedback from mentors, instructors, or professionals working in the IT industry. They can provide valuable insights and perspectives on your skills and knowledge. Ask for constructive feedback regarding your technical proficiency, problem-solving abilities, communication skills, and other relevant areas. Their feedback will help you gain a more comprehensive understanding of your strengths and areas where you can further develop your expertise.

By evaluating your existing skills and knowledge related to IT, you gain a clear understanding of your strengths and areas for improvement. This assessment will guide your decisions as you embark on your IT career journey, helping you identify areas where you need to bridge gaps or acquire additional knowledge. It will also assist you in setting realistic goals for professional development and guide your choices regarding further education, certifications, or specialized training. Remember, the evaluation process is dynamic, and as you gain more experience and expertise, you should regularly reassess your skills to stay relevant and competitive in the rapidly evolving IT industry.

1.6. *Determine any Gaps in Your Skill-set and Areas for Improvement:*

After evaluating your existing skills and knowledge related to IT, the next step is to determine any gaps in your skillset and areas for improvement. Identifying these gaps will help you develop a targeted plan for professional growth and ensure you are equipped with the necessary skills to succeed in your chosen IT career path.

1.7. *Analyze Requirements for Potential Jobs*

Review the job descriptions and requirements for the specific IT roles or positions you are interested in pursuing. Identify the key skills, qualifications, and knowledge that employers are seeking. Compare these requirements to your current skill-set and identify any gaps or areas where you may fall short. This analysis will give you a clear understanding of the skills you need to acquire or enhance to meet the expectations of potential employers.

1.8. *Research Industry Trends:*

Stay updated on the latest trends, technologies, and best practices in the IT industry. Technology is constantly evolving, and new skills and knowledge become in demand. Research industry publications, online forums, and professional networks to identify emerging technologies or areas of expertise that align with your career goals. Determine if there are any gaps in your knowledge or skills related to these emerging trends, and prioritize acquiring them to stay relevant in the rapidly changing IT landscape.

1.9. *Seek Learning Opportunities:*

Once you have identified the specific gaps in your skillset, seek out learning opportunities to address them. This can include enrolling in courses, attending workshops or conferences, participating in Ibinars, or pursuing certifications. Look for reputable educational institutions, online platforms, or industry-recognized programs that offer relevant training. Leverage both formal and informal learning opportunities to acquire the knowledge and skills needed to fill the identified gaps.

1.10. *Seek Mentorship and Guidance*

Mentorship can play a crucial role in identifying and addressing skill gaps. Seek out experienced professionals in the IT industry who can provide guidance, advice, and mentorship. They can help you identify areas for improvement and provide insights on the skills and knowledge that are most valuable in the field. Engage in networking events, join professional associations or online communities to connect with mentors who can support your professional growth.

1.11. *Embrace a Growth Mindset*

Develop a growth mindset and approach learning as a continuous journey. Embrace challenges, view setbacks as opportunities for learning, and be open to feedback. Cultivate a mindset that encourages lifelong learning and continuous improvement. This mindset will enable you to adapt to new technologies, acquire new skills, and stay ahead in the ever-changing IT industry.

1.12. *Conduct Informational Interviews*

Reach out to professionals currently working in the IT industry and request informational interviews. Engage in conversations with individuals who hold positions you are interested in. Ask them about their roles, daily tasks, career paths, and the skills required to excel in their field. This firsthand information will provide valuable insights and help you make informed decisions about the IT career paths you wish to pursue.

1.13. *Utilize Online Resources*

Leverage online resources such as industry websites,

professional forums, blogs, and career websites to gather information about different IT career paths. These resources often offer detailed descriptions of job roles, salary ranges, industry trends, and potential growth opportunities. Stay updated with the latest industry news and developments to understand the evolving landscape of IT careers.

1.14. *Seek Guidance from Career Counselors or Mentors*

Engage with career counselors or mentors who specialize in the IT field. They can provide personalized guidance and advice based on your interests, skills, and career goals. They can help you explore different IT career paths, evaluate their suitability to your strengths, and provide insights into emerging job roles and future industry trends.

1.15. *Consider Your Long-Term Goals*

Reflect on your long-term aspirations and goals within the IT industry. Consider whether you prefer a technical path, a managerial role, or a blend of both. Determine if you have an inclination towards entrepreneurship, research, or specialized expertise. Understanding your long-term goals will help you narrow down your choices and focus on the career paths that align with your aspirations.

By thoroughly researching various IT career paths and job roles, you can gain a comprehensive understanding of the opportunities available to you. This research will enable you to make informed decisions about the specialization you wish to pursue and the skills you need to develop. Keep in mind that the IT industry is dynamic, with new roles emerging and existing roles evolving over time. Stay open to exploring new paths and continuously update your knowledge as technology advances. Your research will serve as a strong foundation for your IT career journey and help you navigate towards success in your chosen field.

1.16. *Industry Outlook*

Research the overall industry outlook for different IT fields. Look for reports, studies, and market analyses that provide insights into the growth projections and trends within the IT industry. Assess the sectors that are experiencing rapid expansion and high demand for skilled professionals. Consider the factors driving this growth, such as emerging technologies, digital transformation, data analytics, cybersecurity concerns, or advancements in artificial intelligence.

1.17. *Salary and Compensation*

Consider the salary and compensation packages associated with different IT fields. Research the average salaries, bonuses, and benefits offered to professionals in various roles. Compare the earning potential across different IT specializations and identify the fields that offer competitive compensation packages. Keep in mind that salary ranges can vary depending on factors such as experience, location, industry, and specific job requirements.

1.18. *Emerging Technologies and Trends*

Stay informed about emerging technologies and trends that are shaping the IT industry. Identify areas that are experiencing rapid growth and adoption, such as cloud computing, machine learning, blockchain, Internet of Things (IoT), or augmented reality. Assess the demand for professionals with expertise in these technologies and consider their long-term growth potential.

1.19. *Skill Transferability and Flexibility*

Assess the transferability and flexibility of skills across different IT fields. Determine if the skills you acquire in a particular specialization can be applied to other related areas. This flexibility allows you to adapt to changing market demands and explore new opportunities within the IT industry without starting from scratch.

By considering the demand and growth potential of different IT fields, you can make informed decisions about the areas that offer promising career prospects. This assessment will help you align your skills, interests, and long-term goals with the fields that are expected to experience sustained growth and high demand for IT professionals. HoIver, it's important to strike a balance betIen market demand and your personal passion and interests to ensure a fulfilling and rewarding IT career.

1.20. *Continuously Adapt and Evolve*

Keep in mind that your interests and skills may evolve over time. The IT industry is dynamic and constantly evolving, with new technologies and career opportunities emerging. Stay open to exploring new areas and be willing to adapt and acquire new skills as needed. Continuously seek learning opportunities and stay updated with industry trends to remain relevant in your chosen IT career path.

Chapter 4: Choose your Path

Building a solid groundwork for a prosperous IT profession begins with getting the appropriate training and credentials. Maintaining your credibility, expanding your network, and showcasing your dedication to professional development all depend on keeping abreast of developments in your field and earning industry-recognized qualifications. In this chapter we will examine some important things to think about when you plan your IT career courses and certifications.

1.1. *Determine Necessary Competencies*

Find out what courses and credentials are needed for your desired IT profession. Depending on the job, you may need a certain degree or certification to get hired. Determine what skills and experiences are required to enter and progress in the field. Think about whether a industry or technology certification and/or four-year college degree is required, a master's degree is preferable, or whether you can learn what you need through a online course, or intensive training program called a boot-camp.

1.2. Pick a Respected Degree Program

Verify the accreditation and reputation of any degree offering schools you are thinking about applying. With proper accreditation, students may rest assured that their education will be valuable and respected in the job market. Seek out institutions with well-respected IT degree programs.

Think about going to school for something like Data Science, Software Engineering, or Computer Science. Earning a degree demonstrates that you have mastered the field's most fundamental ideas and theories. It shows that you are willing to put in the time and effort required in the classroom, and it can provide you an edge in the employment market.

1.3. Look into Your IT Certification Courses

Find a recognized IT Certification courses that will help you get where you want to go in your chosen field. You can prove your competence in a particular field by earning a certification.

1.4. Think About Online Immersive Training

Learning new skills and expanding your knowledge base has never been more convenient than with online courses and boot-camps. Numerous IT-related courses taught by professionals are available online. Bootcamps are short-term, intensive training programs that aim to teach specific, industry-relevant skills. Before committing to one of these programs, you should investigate its history, syllabus, and alumni results.

1.5. Explore Educational and Training Options

Find ways to further your education and credentials outside of the classroom. Participate in events such as seminars, workshops, and conferences that are relevant to your interests. Participate in online networks and forums within your field to learn about new developments, best practices, and technology as they emerge. Take part in open-source projects to build your skill-set and your network in the real world.

1.6. *Never Stop Studying*

It is important to keep in mind that education in the IT area is a never-ending cycle. Rapid technological development also results in the frequent emergence of novel resources and approaches. Adopt a growth mentality and maintain a genuine interest in the latest developments in your chosen area of IT. Keep your knowledge of your field fresh by regularly reading up on relevant periodicals, blogs, podcasts, and online resources.

To succeed in the information technology field, it is essential to have the education and credentials in that field. Getting a degree or certification will increase your marketability to potential employers and help you climb the career ladder. Keeping up with the rapidly developing IT field requires a combination of classroom knowledge, hands-on experience, and a dedication to lifelong learning.

Chapter 5: Equip Yourself

One of the most important things you can do for your IT profession is to get some hands-on experience. It provides an opportunity to put what you have learned into practice, grow in important ways, and show what you can do to prospective employers. This chapter will cover how to set you up for success and some important things to keep in mind when looking for internships or jobs in the IT field.

1.1. *Cooperative Education and Internships*

Look into cooperative education and internship opportunities at local businesses, nonprofits, and universities. Work on real projects and team up with experts in the field with the help of these programs that offer invaluable hands-on experience. Internships and co-op work allow you to put what you have learned in the classroom into practice while gaining valuable work experience and guidance from seasoned professionals.

1.2. *Service to Others and Non-Profit Groups*

Think about giving back to the community by lending your IT

knowledge and talents to a non-profit, an open-source project, or a community effort. You may improve your technical skills while helping worthy causes with these experiences. The act of volunteering not only benefits the society, but also highlights personal qualities such as initiative and teamwork.

1.3. *Independent Work and Initiatives*

Take on some freelancing or side projects to increase your resume's breadth and depth. Provide your expertise in areas like web development, software customization, and technical support to small businesses and individuals. To gain experience in a variety of fields, practice customer management, and showcase your abilities, consider freelancing.

1.4. *Connections and guidance*

Create a solid network of contacts in the business side of IT. Connect with other professionals and broaden your network by participating in industry events, conferences, and meetups. Meet with seasoned professionals who are willing to guide your professional development as mentors. Developing your network can lead to better internships, paid positions, and even long-term professional partnerships.

1.5. *Experimentation and Individual Work*

Develop your knowledge and experience with IT by taking on personal projects. Create Internet sites, code programs, and play around with new platforms. Personal projects are a great way to display your problem-solving and initiative skills, in addition to giving you a chance to follow your passions. They can be used as proof that you can see a project through from start to finish, as well as examples of your work.

1.6. *Learning on the Job and Accreditation*

Keep abreast of what is happening in the IT world by constantly expanding your knowledge. Take advantage of the many opportunities for hands-on learning and practical application provided via online courses, workshops, and professional certifications. Not only will your knowledge expand, but so will your ability to apply it, thanks to the exercises and projects included in these courses.

1.7. Gain Wisdom

Think on the things you have done in the real world and draw wisdom from those. Examine the problems you encountered, the steps you took to fix them, and the insights you gained. Adopt a coachable attitude by actively seeking out feedback from superiors, mentors, and coworkers. A well-rounded IT professional is one who takes in criticism and uses it to grow in knowledge and expertise.

In the IT industry, hands-on experience is crucial. It is a great way to put your knowledge to use, grow as a professional, and impress future employers. Your chances of landing a job in the IT field will improve dramatically if you actively seek and embrace practical experiences, such as internships, volunteering, freelance work, personal projects, or continual learning.

Chapter 6: Develop Your Professional Brand and Portfolio

An effective IT career requires constant learning and networking with other professionals. Opportunities, insights, and promotions can all come through expanding one's professional network and investing in one's own development on a regular basis. Here are some essential tips for advancing your IT career through networking:

1.1. *Create and maintain a network of contacts in your field*

Seek out ways to meet other IT professionals and build your network. You can meet professionals, experts, and possible mentors at events like conferences and seminars. Participate in industry-specific forums and join groups on social media to network with other professionals and learn about the latest developments. Make an effort to get to know people, join in conversations, and lend a helping hand when you can.

1.2. Make use of many online mediums

Use social media sites to network with other professionals, join relevant organizations, and disseminate your knowledge in your field. Establish yourself as an authority in your field by exhibiting your work and actively participating in online discussions. Networking, knowledge exchange, and maintaining professional connections are all greatly facilitated by social media.

1.3. Participate in Group Activities

Take part in IT-related workshops, webinars, and gatherings. These gatherings provide chances to pick the brains of leaders in one's field, discover the latest developments in one's field, and network with other professionals. Take part in the conversation, pose questions, and share your thoughts. In addition to meeting interesting people, you might find a mentor or form a partnership by networking at these events.

1.4. *Find a Mentor or Mentoring Program*

Find a mentor among established experts in your area. An able mentor can help you grow professionally by pointing you in the right direction and giving you sound advise based on their own experiences. Find a mentoring program through your company, trade group, or internet forum. Also, give some thought to taking on the role of a mentor yourself. Your leadership abilities and your circle of contacts will both benefit from your willingness to share what you have learned with others.

1.5. *Developing Knowledge and Abilities Permanently*

To keep up with the ever-changing IT business, it is important to invest in your own education and professional growth. Take advantage of online courses, certificates, and seminars to learn about cutting-edge equipment, software, and processes. Find courses that fill in the knowledge or experience gaps you have identified. In order to keep up with the latest developments and standard practices in your field, make it a habit to read relevant publications, subscribe to relevant blogs, and research credible web resources.

1.6. *Participate in Open Source Initiatives*

Collaborate with other developers, hone your problem-solving abilities, and broaden your professional network by taking part in or contributing to open-source projects. These group efforts let you put your skills to use solving real-world problems while gaining valuable experience and networking with others. Participating in such pursuits indicates enthusiasm, commitment, and teamwork skills.

1.7. *Seek Opinions and Evaluate Your Progress*

You can learn a lot about your skills and opportunities for growth by actively seeking feedback from your managers, mentors, and coworkers. Accept and learn from criticism that helps you improve. It is important to take stock of your professional development on a regular basis, evaluate your achievements, and formulate fresh objectives in light of the results. Your career and social connections will benefit from your consistent efforts to better yourself.

Both networking and professional development are never-ending endeavors that necessitate dedication and time. You

may advance your career, remain relevant in your field, and prove your worth as a contributor to the IT sector by cultivating and expanding your professional network, engaging in lifelong learning, and actively seeking mentorship and feedback.

Chapter 7: Excel in your Job Search and Interview

To succeed in today's competitive job market and land your ideal job or take your career to the next level, you need to put out your best effort at every step of the hiring process. A combination of preparation, confidence, and good communication is required to master the basic tasks of finding a job, interviewing well, and negotiating a salary. In this chapter, you will learn effective methods for doing a job search, acing an interview, and successfully negotiating a job offer.

1.1. *Stand Out in the Job Market*

Start by taking stock of your experience, aptitudes, and long-term goals to determine where you want your career to go. Define your ideal employer and career role, and focus your job search efforts.

1.1.1. *Making a Winning Resume and Cover Letter*

Create an eye-catching resume and cover letter that truly reflects your background and tailored to each job application. To make the right impression, be sure to emphasize your relevant qualifications and past successes. Always use action verbs and provide numbers to back up your claims of success.

Build and use your existing professional network, show up at relevant events, and make use of digital tools to meet new people and continue to build your professional network. Take advantage of mentorship and informational interviews.

1.2. *Strategies for Finding a Job Online*

To find a job online, you can use job boards, professional networking sites, and company websites. Prepare yourself by creating and saving a job search on sites such as Linkedin.com, Indeed.com, careerbuilder.com, etc. and turn on job notifications. In addition, research potential employers to find the best fit.

1.2.1. *Shine during the Interview*

Do your homework on the company and learn everything you can about its history, values, goals, and recent successes as well as the industry as a whole. Take advantage of this knowledge to impress the interviewer with your energy and motivation.

Anticipate and practice answering typical interview questions with clear and well-organized explanations. Make use of the Situation, Task, Action, and Result (STAR) format to highlight your relevant work history and achievements.

1.2.2. *Exhibiting Your Capabilities*

Showcase your expertise in technical areas, industry knowledge, and interpersonal abilities throughout the interview. Describe in detail how you have applied these talents to prior positions with positive outcomes.

Prove that you are a good fit for the company's culture by demonstrating that you can work well with others and adapt to new situations. Talk on how your shared beliefs and work experiences align with those of the company.

Think about the organization, the team, and the position to which you are applying, and make a list of questions to ask.

Show your interviewer your interest and curiosity by having a meaningful dialogue with them.

Dress properly, make and maintain eye contact, and exude confidence in your body language to make a good impression throughout the interview. Pay close attention to the interviewer's body language and engage in active listening.

1.3. *Successfully Negotiating Your Job Offer*

Examine market averages, pay ranges, and benefits packages for comparable positions to get a sense of what you should be making. Make use of wage calculators and market research to strengthen your bargaining position. Realize how much you are worth based on your education, experience, and accomplishments. Draw attention to your special skills and the value you may bring to the table during negotiations. Find out what pay and benefits you are hoping for. Think on things that do not involve money, such chances to advance your career or get more time off.

1.3.1. *Communicate your needs and the reasoning*

State clearly the salary you want. You should back up your demands with evidence of why you should get what you want from the company, such as your skills, experience, and market value.

Your goal should be a win-win situation for both parties. Be flexible and willing to consider new options in order to find a solution that works for everyone involved. Look at the income, perks, vacation time, and possibility for advancement, before making a decision. If there is any doubt, you should get it cleared up before making a choice.

Job hunting, interviews, and negotiations are all crucial skills for climbing the corporate ladder. By showcasing your proficiency in these areas, you will set yourself apart from the competition, boost your chances of landing your dream job, and strengthen your hand when negotiating your salary. Always make sure you are well-prepared, confident, and communicating clearly before taking any action.

To keep up with today's competitive employment market, it is important to constantly hone your abilities and look for ways to advance professionally.

Chapter 8: Thrive in Your Career

In the dynamic field of IT, staying current with industry trends and adapting to new technologies and methodologies is crucial for long-term success. The rapid pace of technological advancements necessitates a commitment to continuous learning and a willingness to adapt. In this chapter, we will explore some key considerations for staying current and ahead of the competition.

1.1. *Embrace Lifelong Learning*

Commit to lifelong learning and make it a priority to stay updated with the latest developments in your field. Subscribe to industry publications, follow influential blogs, and join relevant online communities. Actively seek out learning opportunities, whether through formal certification courses, webinars, or self-paced online resources. Stay curious and open-minded, and consistently seek to expand your knowledge base.

1.2. *Attend Industry Conferences and Events*

Participate in industry conferences, seminars, and events to gain insights into emerging technologies and industry best practices. These gatherings provide opportunities to learn from experts, network with peers, and engage in discussions that drive innovation. Stay informed about upcoming events and prioritize attending those that align with your interests and career goals.

1.3. *Join Professional Associations and Communities*

Become a member of professional associations and communities in your area of expertise. These organizations often provide access to valuable resources, networking opportunities, and industry-specific insights. Engage in discussions, share your knowledge, and learn from others. Active participation in professional associations can help you stay current and build connections within the industry.

1.4. *Embrace Online Learning Platform*

Leverage online learning platform to access a wide range of courses and tutorials. Many platforms offer a diverse selection of IT-related courses taught by industry experts. Explore topics that are relevant to your career and leverage these platforms to up-skill or re-skill as needed. Online learning provides flexibility, allowing you to learn at your own pace and fit learning into your busy schedule.

Take advantage of opportunities for continuous professional development. Seek out internal training programs and attend workshops offered by your organization or industry partners. Look for certifications or specialized training programs that align with your career goals. By actively investing in your professional development, you stay relevant and adaptable in an ever-changing IT landscape.

1.5. *Stay Abreast of Industry Trends*

Keep a close eye on industry trends and emerging technologies. Stay informed about advancements in areas such as artificial intelligence, cloud computing, cybersecurity, and data analytics. Follow influential thought leaders, subscribe to industry newsletters, and engage in discussions on social media platforms. Understanding industry trends allows you to anticipate changes, identify new opportunities, and make informed career decisions.

Embrace new technologies and methodologies that shape the IT industry. Stay flexible and open to learning new tools, programming languages, frameworks, and methodologies. Embrace the agile mindset and be willing to adapt your approach and workflows as needed. The ability to quickly learn and adapt to new technologies and methodologies positions you as a valuable asset to employers and opens up new career opportunities.

1.6. *Cultivate a Growth Mindset*

Adopt a growth mindset that embraces challenges, learns from failures, and seeks continuous improvement. Embrace change and see it as an opportunity for growth and innovation. Be willing to step out of your comfort zone and explore new areas of IT. Continuously seek feedback, reflect on your experiences, and apply lessons learned to enhance your skills and capabilities.

1.7. *Build a Diverse Professional Network*

Expand your professional network to include individuals from diverse backgrounds, experiences, and areas of expertise. Engage with professionals outside of your immediate domain to gain fresh perspectives and insights. Building a diverse network provides access to a wide range of knowledge and fosters collaborative opportunities.

1.8. *Stay agile and Develop problem-solving skills*

Be willing to experiment, iterate, and pivot as needed. Embrace agile methodologies that promote flexibility and responsiveness to changing requirements and market demands. Cultivate a problem-solving mindset that enables you to approach challenges with creativity and resourcefulness. Continuously refine your analytical and critical thinking skills to tackle complex problems effectively.

Seek opportunities to work with professionals from different disciplines and departments. Embracing cross-functional collaboration enhances your ability to adapt to diverse perspectives, workstyles, and approaches.

1.9. *Seek feedback* a*nd reflect*

Regularly seek feedback from colleagues, mentors, and supervisors. Reflect on your experiences and identify areas for improvement. Actively incorporate feedback to enhance your skills and adapt your approach as needed.

1.10. *Maintain a growth mindset*

Continuously monitor market trends, industry disruptions, and emerging technologies. Anticipate shifts in demand and skills requirements, and proactively acquire the necessary knowledge and skills to stay relevant. Strive for continuous improvement in all aspects of your work. Regularly evaluate your performance, seek opportunities for growth, and take steps to refine your skills and capabilities.

Embrace the belief that your abilities can be developed through dedication and hard work. Embrace challenges as learning opportunities and maintain a curiosity-driven approach to expand your knowledge and skill set.

By staying current and adapting to changes, you position yourself as a valuable asset in the rapidly evolving IT industry. Embracing a mindset of continuous learning and adaptability not only enhances your career prospects, but also fuels your professional growth and success in the ever-evolving work environment.

Most importantly, have an attitude of gratitude, live and enjoy every moment, while you plan and prepare for the future. Maintain a positive attitude in the face of challenges and setbacks. A positive mindset fosters resilience, motivates others, and helps create a supportive work environment conducive to growth and adaptation.

Congratulations on reaching the end of this life-altering book, and as you move forward in your activities, keep in mind the importance of tapping into your full potential to build a life of amazing depth and breadth. Are you ready to begin?

For additional guidance and support, contact: info@samsonna.com.

About the Author

As a seasoned Technology Leader with a passion for value creation, Shahdrick brings over 18 years of progressive experience in transforming organizations. With an extensive and diverse background that spans across the Corporate, Government, and Professional Services sectors, he stands out as a dynamic and accomplished executive. His expertise shines in the realms of Banking, Financial Services, Healthcare, Technology, and the Public Sector.

Throughout his career, he has collaborated closely with clients of all levels, including Senior Management and CxOs, to drive large-scale IT initiatives to achieve desired outcomes such as increased efficiency, revenue growth, cost reduction, and risk management.

Shahdrick's ability to craft effective strategies, design innovative solution architectures, and build robust applications has consistently optimized global operations, market offerings, and client delivery. His unique skill set enables him to leverage cutting-edge technologies such as Artificial Intelligence (AI), multi-cloud infrastructures, Software-as-a-Service (SaaS) applications, and information security to drive productivity enhancements that have had a significant impact on his clients' multi-billion dollar operations.

His expertise extends beyond the corporate world. He has shared his knowledge as a guest lecturer at many renowned institutions, and has presented at academic conferences and industry events. His insightful industry insights, whitepapers, scholarly reports and recently co-authored a textbook in collaboration with the Johns Hopkins University and World Scientific Publishing, which further solidifies his thought leadership.

Leverage Mr. Samson's proven experience and discover how he can propel you and your organization to new heights. Benefit from his profound understanding of business, technology, digital disruption, and growth strategies.

Resources

IT Training, Career Counseling and Job Assistance:

1. Samsons Training Services, (www.samsonna.com): Training in hot areas such as AI/Robotics, IT Management, Software Programming, Network Engineering, Healthcare Technology, Project Management, Mobile Development, Cybersecurity, and more! Live instruction, hybrid, and self-paced courses available. Additionally, scholarships, apprenticeship, internships, and support services, if available at the time of application.

Reference

1. Goldman Sachs. (2023). Generative AI could raise global GDP by 7 percent. Retrieved from https://www.goldmansachs.com/intelligence/pages/generative-ai-could-raise-global-gdp-by-7-percent.html

2. Accenture. (2019, June 11). Failure to Scale Artificial Intelligence Could Put 75 Percent of Organizations Out of Business, Accenture Study Shows. Retrieved from https://newsroom.accenture.com/news/failure-to-scale-artificial-intelligence-could-put-75-percent-of-organizations-out-of-business-accenture-study-shows.htm

Are You Ready?

Made in the USA
Middletown, DE
23 June 2023

33339750R00060